THE WORLD'S MOST AMAZING
MONSTER FACTS

For Kids

First published in Great Britain in 2003
by Egmont Books Limited,
239 Kensington High Street,
London W8 6SA

Copyright © 2003 Egmont Books Limited

ISBN 0 603 56104 7

1 3 5 7 9 10 8 6 4 2

Printed and bound in the U.A.E.

THE WORLD'S MOST AMAZING
MONSTER FACTS

For Kids

Written and compiled by Guy Campbell & Mark Devins
Illustrated by Paul Moran

CONTENTS

THE VAMPIRE STRIKES BACK

The Real Count Dracula

The rugged Transylvanian Alps provide one of the most spectacular landscapes in Europe. Hawks soar around the snow-covered mountain peaks and bears stalk the forests below. Medieval villages and the ruins of mighty castles can abruptly appear through the fog.

Transylvania also produced a leader known as a defender of the Christian faith, a Romanian hero, and a subhuman monster. His name was Prince Vlad, but the world knows him by another name: Dracula.

Vlad was born in 1431 into a noble family. His father was called "Dracul," meaning "dragon" or "devil" in Romanian, because he belonged to the Order of the Dragon, a Christian group at war with the Muslim Ottoman Empire. "Dracula" means "son of Dracul'", but also "son of the devil". Scholars believe this nickname was probably the source of the legend of Dracula.

He grew up in an unstable and dangerous world, his country constantly at war. Dracula's father was murdered, while his older brother, Mircea, was blinded with red-hot iron stakes and buried alive by his enemies.

From 1448 until his death in 1476, Dracula ruled Walachia and Transylvania, both part of Romania today. The church praised him for defending Christianity, but disapproved of his cruel methods, which became infamous.

Dracula earned another nickname, "Vlad Tepes", which means "Vlad the Impaler". Dracula's favourite method of torture was to throw people onto wooden stakes and leave them to writhe in agony, often for days. As a warning to others, the bodies would remain on the stakes as vultures and crows ate the rotting flesh.

During one battle with the Turks, Dracula retreated into nearby mountains, impaling captured people as he went. The Turkish advance was halted because the sultan could not bear the stench from the decaying corpses.

The British newspaper *The Daily Telegraph* reported on Halloween 2000 that Ottomar Rudolphe Vlad Dracula Prince Kretzulesco was looking for a medieval castle in England where he could live and work. Born Otto Berbig, the Prince was adopted by the late Princess Katharina Olympia Caradja, a direct descendant of Dracula himself.

Dracula was reported to have eaten a meal on a table set up amidst hundreds of impaled victims. He was also reported to have occasionally eaten bread dipped in a victim's blood.

Nicholas of Modrussa, Papal envoy in Buda (now Budapest), Hungary, wrote to Pope Pius II that Dracula had massacred 40,000 men, women and children of all ages and nationalities in one incident in 1464. Gabriele Rangone, bishop of Erlau, stated in 1475 that Dracula had personally ordered the murders of 100,000 people, or close to one-fifth of the population under his rule.

Dracula was killed in December 1476 fighting the Turks near Bucharest, Romania. His head was cut off and displayed in the city of Constantinople. He was buried at the Snagov Monastery

near Bucharest. The monastery was also used as a prison and torture chamber, where unsuspecting prisoners praying before an icon of the Virgin Mary would fall through a trapdoor onto sharp stakes below.

In 1931 archaeologists searching Snagov found a coffin covered in a purple shroud embroidered with gold. The skeleton inside was covered with silk brocade, matching a shirt depicted in an old painting of Dracula. A ring, matching those worn by the Order of the Dragon, was sewn into a shirtsleeve.

The contents of the coffin were taken to the History Museum in Bucharest but have since disappeared without a trace, leaving the mysteries of the real Prince Dracula unanswered.

Romania's former Communist dictator, Nicolae Ceauşescu, admired Dracula and portrayed

him as a national hero, downplaying his atrocities. The 500th anniversary of Dracula's death was observed in 1976 with various celebrations, including a commemorative postage stamp.
In 1989, when the Ceauşescu regime was toppled and mobs in Bucharest attempted to storm the government, the dictator and his wife fled to their palace near Snagov, where Dracula was buried.
The Ceauşescus were captured and shot by a firing squad near Dracula's castle.

Belief in vampires and the power of blood is as old as mankind. Early man smeared himself in blood and sometimes drank it. The ancient Chinese, Egyptians, Babylonians, Greeks, and Romans all believed in vampires. The Jewish Talmud tells of Lilith, Adam's disobedient first wife, who was transformed into a monster roaming the night.

Some doctors believe that old peasant tales of aristocratic "vampires" living in nearby castles could be based on medical fact. Some of the traits attributed to vampires – sensitivity to light, fangs, pale skin – may describe the symptoms of certain illnesses. For example, the hereditary blood disease porphyria was believed to be rife among the Eastern European aristocracy. People with porphyria become extremely sensitive to light, develop skin lesions, and get brown or reddish teeth. Physicians at the time sometimes told patients to drink blood from other people to build up their strength.

Rabies, which is spread by animals such as wolves or bats (both associated with vampires), may also have been endemic in Transylvania in Dracula's day. Rabies symptoms include insomnia, madness and hallucinations. Modern treatment for rabies includes immune globulin, a protein found in blood.

In Transylvania, with its blend of Hungarian, Romanian and gypsy folklore, belief in vampires has always been strong. Orthodox Christians believe the soul does not leave the body for the afterlife until 40 days after burial. When an Orthodox Christian is thrown out of the Church, or converts to another faith, it is said that the earth will no longer receive his body, forcing him to wander the Earth undead.

In the Americas, the early Indians of Peru believed in devil worshippers who sucked the life-blood from sleeping youths, while the Aztecs sacrificed victims to ensure the Sun would continue to rise, removing the still-beating hearts from their victims and offering them up to the gods as a gift.

Vampire bats have fewer teeth than other bats because they don't have to chew their food.

LEAPING LIZARDS!

The Komodo Dragon

Komodo Dragons are no myth. They are huge, brown-grey lizards with powerful jaws, razor-sharp claws, and long tails. They have rounded snouts and curved, serrated teeth like a shark's. Movable joints and plates in their skulls enable them to shift their jaws so they can swallow large prey. Komodo Dragons can locate prey from several miles away by smelling it out with sensors on their long, forked tongues. The record size for a Komodo Dragon is more than three metres in length and 165 kilograms in weight.

There are over 3,000 lizard species in the world, and the Komodo Dragon, or

Varanus komodoensis, is the biggest. Its ancestors date back more than 100 million years. They live only on four remote Indonesian islands: Flores, Gili Motang, Komodo and Rinca, and are listed as a vulnerable species by the World Conservation Union. Around 5,000 of these animals exist today.

Komodo Dragons eat carrion (dead animal flesh) but also prey on deer, wild pigs, snakes, monkeys, livestock including goats and even buffalo and wild horses. Scientists believe that millions of years ago, Komodo Dragons hunted now-extinct Pygmy Elephants. Young Dragons feed on rodents, insects, lizards, birds, and their eggs.

An adult Dragon will hide along a trail and wait for an unsuspecting creature to walk by. Then, with long claws and short, sharp teeth, the Dragon attacks. If the prey escapes, the Dragon will simply follow it at a leisurely pace. That's because saliva in the Dragon's

bite contains a deadly bacteria that will eventually poison its intended meal. Once caught, prey is pinned down with a mighty claw and ripped to pieces by the Dragon's awesome jaws and teeth. After eating something big like a deer, a Dragon will sleep it off for up to a week.

Komodo Dragons have mouths full of flat, serrated teeth, highly adapted for cutting flesh. The teeth break off easily and are replaced frequently: a Dragon may grow as many as 200 new teeth each year.

Komodo Island is a national park set aside for the Dragons' protection. The Dragons used to be allowed to attack goats as a tourist attraction, but this activity was stopped in 1993 because it reduced the lizards' fear of humans, increasing the chances of a Dragon turning man-eater and eating the tourists for breakfast – something which has happened once or twice already.

Life for a young Komodo Dragon is no picnic. As soon as the baby hatches, it scrambles out of the nest and scurries up the nearest tree so it won't be eaten by its own mum and dad. Fortunately for the babies, the adults are too heavy to climb trees. The baby Dragons live in the branches eating eggs, grasshoppers and beetles until they are about four years old and a metre or so long, when they are big enough to look after themselves on the ground.

The Western world did not learn about these Dragons until 1912, when a pilot crash-landed near one of the islands. Since then, human settlements have put pressure on their habitat, but the population has remained stable, and the mighty lizards have become a lucrative tourist attraction, boosting the island economy.

IF YOU GO DOWN TO THE WOODS TODAY

Bigfoot: Half Man, Half Ape

In many remote areas of the world there have been sightings of a hair-covered, man-like creature. It is known by many names, and often claimed as being the "missing link" in evolution between the ape and the primitive human being. In the northwestern USA, this beast is known as "Bigfoot".

There are numerous sightings every year, even today. The descriptions of the creatures are very similar from sighting to sighting. Witnesses have reported the creatures to be anything from one and a half metres to two and a half metres tall.

Bigfoot is far from being confined to North America. He is found in almost all parts of the world, and known by many names.

One of the most famous American Bigfoot sightings took place in the mid 1850s. Two trappers were camping in the woods. Returning to their camp one day, they found it ransacked, and massive footprints on the ground. The men, a little shaken, repaired their camp and got ready for supper.

The only rational – if a little unlikely – explanation the hunters could come up with for the footprints was that they were made by a huge bear walking on its hind legs. They concluded that no human could possibly have made them. One of the men was awakened that night by the sounds of an

intruder. He saw a large figure at the entrance of their home-made shelter, and he could smell a foul smell. He grabbed his rifle and fired. The thing ran back to the woods. The trappers stayed awake for the rest of the night but there were no further visitations.

They continued setting out their traps the next day, staying close together for safety. When they returned to camp, it had been ransacked again. More two-legged footprints were found.

The men made a large fire and took turns guarding camp. Well into the night, the thing came back. They could hear it as it walked around the woods near the camp, making strange growling noises but it never came near their fire.

The next day the trappers decided, not surprisingly, to move on. All morning they stayed together, collecting up their traps from the day before. Both had the feeling of being watched, and they could hear twigs snapping in the woods nearby. Around noon, one left the other to return and pack up their camp.

When the second hunter returned with the traps in the late afternoon, a horrifying sight greeted him. His friend lay dead, his neck broken and four fang marks in his throat. More footprints were at the scene. That was it. The remaining trapper left everything behind. He didn't stop running until he got back to civilization.

In some parts of the US, the apeman is called Sasquatch. In various parts of Europe, he is known as Kaptar, Biabin-guli, Grendel, Ferla Mohir or Brenin Ilwyd. In Africa: Ngoloko or Kikomba. In Asia: Gin-sung, Mirygdy, Mecheny, Nguoi Rung or Yeti, and in Australia, the Yowie.

IT'S A DOG'S LIFE

The Facts about Werewolves

It is believed that humans and wolves evolved at around the same time: approximately 10,000 years BC.

In Greek myth, Lycaos was the extraordinarily cruel king of Arcadia. Lycaos sought favour with the great god Zeus by offering him the flesh of a young child. Enraged, Zeus turned Lycaos into a wolf. Over the centuries, the belief that certain people can turn themselves into animals – especially wolves – and roam the earth doing evil, became widespread.

In 400 BC, Damarchus, a supposed werewolf from Arcadia, was reported to have won boxing medals at the Olympic Games.

In the Middle Ages, many Europeans believed wolves were tools of the devil, and the animals were ruthlessly hunted. Epileptics and the mentally ill were often brought to court and accused of being werewolves. Between 1520 and 1630 there were over 30,000 werewolf trials in France alone.

In the year AD 930 Pope Leon was informed of two sorceresses in Germany who could transform others into animals. One of their victims was able to regain his human form by eating roses.

Today, psychologists use the term "lycanthrope" to describe a mentally ill person who actually believes he has been changed into an animal.

Werewolves supposedly love to eat babies and corpses.

The word "werewolf" means "manwolf" since "wer" is the Saxon word for man.

In mythology, silver bullets or arrows can kill a werewolf, but it is not guaranteed.

After death, a werewolf is said to resume his human identity.

It is believed that a werewolf waking as a human will still bear any wounds he or she acquired while in the werewolf state.

When someone changes into a werewolf, they are supposed to lose all control over their human mind and develop all the senses and thoughts of a wolf.

When a werewolf changes back into a human, he is supposed have no recollection of the previous night's events.

The first werewolf movie was called
The Werewolf of London and was
released in 1935.

**In Italy, the belief is that anybody born
under a full moon on a Friday is likely to
become a werewolf.**

Werewolf hunters believe that you can get
away from a werewolf and be safe by
climbing up an ash tree.

**Other popular beliefs are that werewolves
turn into vampires after death, or that
they are immortal. Vampire experts
disagree!**

The Middle Ages saw a peak in werewolf
reports. In France between 1520 and 1630,
over 30,000 *loup-garou* (werewolf) trials
took place.

THEY STALK THE EARTH!

Actual Sightings of Freaky Creatures!

The Abominable Snowman

Known as "Metch-Kangmi" in Tibet, this is a huge, hairy creature that walks the Himalayas. For decades, explorers have reported huge footprints in the snow. An expedition on Mount Annapurna in 1970 spotted a large, furry creature walking on two legs on a nearby mountain. Climbers watched through binoculars for half an hour before it vanished in a clump of trees. Scientists believe bears could have left some of the footprints. However, the Sherpa people of the region have traditionally believed that the Himalayas are haunted by demons and spirits, while the Yeti, an ancient beast, prowls the mountains.

Amali

From the 1870s onwards, an English explorer named Alfred Smith spent a good deal of time in central Africa. In a memoir entitled, *TraderHorn*, he mentioned two animals, described by local villagers, that met no description of anything he'd ever heard of.

He wrote: "The 'Jago-Nini' they say is still in the swamps and rivers, and I've seen the 'Amali's' footprints, they are about the size of a frying pan in circumference and with three claws instead of five."

In the 1970s, American herpetologist (reptile expert) James Powell was conducting field research in Gabon, Africa. When he showed pictures of various animals to native informants, they most often compared the Amali to the Diplodocus, a long-necked sauropod dinosaur.

The Beast of Bodmin

This cat-like creature was thought responsible for the death of over 200 farm animals over a five-month period in England in 1987. The creature, and others like it, have been sighted numerous times since then and one was once clocked running at over 55 km/h. The beast has also been seen to leap over two-metre-high fences without any difficulty. The most plausible explanation for the Beast is that it is an escaped big cat that is surviving in the wild.

Bunyip

Beginning in the 19th century, all the way through to 1932, an odd creature was often reported to have been seen in Australia. The "Bunyip" was semi-aquatic, bigger than a dog, with long, black hair and no tail. It had a horse-like head and long ears, but was never captured or identified. Today, the word "bunyip" refers to any imaginary, spooky animal that inspires laughter or fear.

Champ

In July 1883, Sheriff Nathan H. Mooney looked out on Lake Champlain in New York state, USA, and saw a gigantic water serpent about 50 metres away. It rose about one and a half metres out of the water, was seven or eight metres long and close enough for the witness to see clearly some round white spots inside its mouth. Lake Champlain's monster is nicknamed "Champ", and has been sighted over 240 times. Champlain is a deep, freshwater lake, created some 10,000 years ago, and supports more than enough fish to feed a small group of lake monsters. The most significant photograph was taken on July 5, 1977 by Sandra Mansi of Connecticut. Mansi took a photo of what she thought was a "dinosaur" whose neck and head were some two metres out of the water. The Mansi photograph had been examined by scientists, who concluded that it has not been retouched or tampered with.

Chupacabras

This deadly killer rears its ugly head periodically in Latin America. Recently, the corpses of 800 animals – sheep, pigs, chicken, and dogs – have been found, drained of blood, in northern Chile. The bodies are invariably covered with strange bite-marks.The monster is described as a winged monkey, about two to two and a half metres tall, with long, clawed arms and hideous fangs. Other eyewitnesses state that the creature resembles a flying rodent or a species of kangaroo.

In 1995, in Puerto Rico, Chupacabras allegedly killed eight sheep at once, leaving behind a pile of bloodless corpses. The beast has also struck in Texas, Costa Rica, and Mexico. Chupacabras could be a cousin of the vampire bat, three species of which live in parts of Mexico, Central and South America.

Duck-billed Platypus

When word of this creature first reached Europe in 1797, everyone thought it was an elaborate hoax. Even when stuffed specimens arrived, people suspected that parts of different animals were all glued together, and when they heard that it was an egg-laying mammal, they laughed even louder. Only when eminent scientists performed on-site observations of the animal in its natural habitat did the rest of the scientific world finally agree it really existed.

Kapre

Persistent reports from the islands of Luzon and Samarlead lead one to believe that Bigfoot has a cousin in the Philippines. Witnesses claim that the Kapre stands two and a half metres tall and is covered with hair. They say its face, hands, and feet are human-like, and it eats fruits, crabs, fish, and the occasional rat.

Loch Ness Monster

In 1933, a man and a woman claimed to have seen a lizard-like creature 12 to 15 metres long holding an animal in its jaws cross over a road and disappear into Loch Ness, Scotland. Nessie is more usually described as a giant creature with a huge, rounded body around 30 metres long, and a long neck. Some think it is a prehistoric sea-going dinosaur, possibly a pleiosaur. An expedition in 1934 at the height of "monster fever" claimed 21 sightings and took five pictures.

Scientists have speculated that Nessie is a large ocean fish, or eel, that has became stranded in the loch. However, Loch Ness is more than 200 metres deep. Little sunlight penetrates its depths, making photosynthesis difficult, so few plants or fish survive there. Although it is 35 kilometres long (the largest freshwater lake in Great Britain) and a monster could easily lurk undetected in the murky depths, the animal would not find much to eat. Since the larger public first became aware of it, the Loch Ness Monster has become an international media star, appearing in numerous movies, and even turning up on a commemorative stamp issued by the Maldive Islands.

De Loys' Ape

This creature was killed on the Venezuela/Columbia border in 1917 by one Francois De Loys and his party. It appears to be a very man-like ape, but has never been identified as a known species. The size and shape of the beast's forehead are unlike that of any of the known primates of South America. Theories as to its identity have suggested that it is a South American version of Bigfoot, or even the missing evolutionary link between human beings and apes.

Frogman of Loveland

This amphibian freak has been seen by numerous people around Loveland, Ohio, USA. Witnesses include police officers who have seen the creatures at the side of the road. Descriptions of the creature all seem to match. It is one to one and a half metres tall, walks upright like a human, has webbed hands and feet, the head of a large frog and leathery skin.

Giant Congo Snake

In 1959 a photograph was taken by a Belgian helicopter pilot, Remy Van Lierde, while on patrol over the Congo. The snake he snapped measured 12 to 15 metres in length, and was brown and green with a white belly. It had triangular jaws and a metre-long head. Experts have verified the pictures as authentic. As the helicopter flew in lower, the snake raised its head up three metres and made as if to strike at the helicopter.

Mapinguary

Hunters in South America's rainforest call it the "beast with the breath of hell". Residents of Brazil's Matto Grosso know it as the "Mapinguary". It is a giant two-legged beast that emits a stench so foul, that those who encounter it are rendered helpless. Zoologists who have studied the reports take them seriously. Some believe the creature to be a hitherto unknown type of ape.

Mawnan Owlman

In the 1970s, a silvery, feathered birdman was observed by people in Mawnan in Cornwall. The birdman was said to have pincers as feet, reddish eyes and a large mouth. Two sisters watched it fly over a church in 1976. In July of that same year there were more sightings of the creature, both on the ground and in the sky. From June to August of 1978 there were additional sightings in the area.

Mermaid

Henry Hudson was a famous English explorer of the 16th century – New York's Hudson River is named after him. He wrote in his journal on June 15, 1610: "This evening one of our company, looking overboard, saw a mermaid, and called up some of the company to see her, one more of the crew came up, and by that time she was close to the ship's side, looking earnestly on the men. A little after a wave came and overturned her."

Mid-east Thunderbird

In 1977, one of two large black birds with two-and-a-half-metre wingspans tried to carry off ten-year-old Marlan Lowe in its claws one evening in Illinois, USA. Although experts say that no bird native to Illinois could possibly lift 31-kilogram Marlan, this is only one of many such encounters with huge black birds in the American Mid-east. They are described as Condor-like in appearance, with white stripes on the neck and massive grasping claws.

Mongolian Death Worm

The Mongolian Death Worm, also known as Allghoi Khorkhoi, was first sighted in 1926 in the Southern Gobi Desert in Mongolia. It is described as a thick-bodied worm between 60 and 120 centimetres long. It is reported to be able to spray an acid-like substance over large prey that causes death instantly. The creature is reported to hibernate during most of the year except for June and July when it becomes very active.

Morag

For centuries there have been reports of a creature dwelling in Loch Morar, just 110 kilometres from Loch Ness. The reports add further to the theory that some giant water-dwelling animals were living in the various lochs as they became land-locked thousands of years ago. Sightings of Morag have been numerous in the 20th century. In 1970, members of the Loch Ness

Investigation Bureau went to investigate the creature in Loch Morar. One member spotted a "hump-shaped object" unlike any normal marine life in the area.

Other Lake Monsters

Monsters have been reported in other lakes around the world, including the Irish Loughs of Ree and Fedda. On Norway's Lake Sudal, a huge creature with a head the size of a rowing boat has been sighted, while a giant red sea horse with a white mane, capable of speeds up to 110 km/h, lurks in Storsjö Lake in Sweden. The monster Ogopogo haunts Canada's Lake Okanagan. New Brunswick, USA has the Lake Utopia Monster; Manipogo haunts Lake Manitoba in Canada; and the Lake Erie monster and the Flathead Lake Monster in Montana, USA, have all attained local fame, some of them long before Nessie came to the world's attention.

Mokele-Mbembe

Could a dinosaur still be alive today in the jungles of the Congo? Since 1913 there have been numerous sightings by local villagers of a creature that resembles a Brontosaurus. Foreigners like Professor Roy P. Mackal have also seen this animal in the Congo. It is about the size of an elephant, with short legs and a long neck. Mokele-Mbembe is herbivorous, but reportedly it has attacked humans.

Mothman

This creature was first spotted in 1966 in Point Pleasant, West Virginia, USA, after numerous UFO sightings. It is described as one and a half to two metres tall, winged and headless, with glowing red eyes on its torso. Mothman has been seen flying across the sky at speeds over 160km/h. As it flies, it emits a high-pitched shriek. The deaths of several small animals and pets have been attributed to the monster.

Orang-Pendek

The Indonesian island of Sumatra is the home of the ape-like Orang-Pendek. It stands one to one and a half metres tall, is covered with dark hair and has a bushy mane. It walks on the ground, and has a footprint like a human's. In 1989, British writer Deborah Martyr made casts of its footprints. The director of the Kerinci Selbat National Park said they were made by no animal he knew of. It is seen fairly often by locals, who say it lives off fruit and small animals.

Poltergeist

German for "knocking ghost", a poltergeist is a noisy supernatural spirit. They are supposed to move furniture, bang on walls and doors and break things to make their presence known. Poltergeists can be aggressive, hurling objects and striking people. They are said to turn up at séances, where they cause trouble.

Queensland Marsupial

This lion/tiger/cat is usually described as a heavy-set animal the size of a large dog with stripes across its back. It has a feline head and a nasty temperament, often taking its temper out on dogs sent out after it. Numerous reports describe it leaping through the air and disembowelling dogs with a swipe of its claws. Other reports indicate that it is a marsupial, with a peculiar hopping gait.

Zuiyo-maru Monster

On April 25, 1977, a fishing boat named the *Zuiyo-maru* was trawling east of Christchurch, New Zealand, when an enormous animal carcass became entangled in its nets. The massive creature, weighing about 9,000 kilograms, was pulled aboard and photographed before being dumped back in the ocean. The beast, resembling a sea-going dinosaur, has yet to be identified.

MONSTERS OF THE DEEP

The Danger that Lurks Beneath

The Giant Squid

The existence of the Giant Squid is well accepted by science, though few have ever been seen, and little is known about its habits.

Giant Squid are carnivorous molluscs that have a long, torpedo-shaped body. At one end, surrounding a vicious beaked mouth strong enough to cut through steel cable, are five pairs of arms. One pair, longer than the rest, are used to catch food and bring it to the mouth. Just past the mouth are the eyes, the largest in the animal kingdom, measuring up to 45 centimetres across.

The Giant Squid moves through the ocean using a jet of water forced out of its body by a siphon. It eats fish and other squid, and mounts terrifying attacks on whales and vessels at sea. The legends of the Kraken, a many-armed sea monster that could pull a whole ship under the water, are probably based on the Giant Squid.

The largest Giant Squid ever measured was discovered at Timble Tickle on November 2, 1878. The body was six metres from tail to beak. The longer tentacles measured over ten metres and were tipped with ten-centimetre suckers.

In 1965, a Soviet whaling ship watched a battle between a Giant Squid and a 40-tonne Sperm Whale. In this case neither was victorious. The strangled whale was found floating in the sea with the squid's tentacles wrapped around its throat. The squid's severed head was found in the whale's stomach.

Sperm Whales eat squid, and originally it had been thought that fights between them were the result of a Sperm Whale taking on a squid that was just too large to be an easy meal. The incident with a ship, the *Brunswick* suggests otherwise ...

The *Brunswick* was a 15,000-tonne auxiliary tanker owned by the Royal Norwegian Navy. In the 1930s it was attacked at least three times by Giant Squid. In each case the squid would pull alongside, swim with the vessel, then suddenly turn and ram into the ship's side, wrapping its tentacles around the hull. The encounters were fatal for the squid. Unable to get a good grip on the ship's steel surface, the monsters slid off and fell into the ship's propellers to a grisly death.

Unfortunately for scientists, but good for the rest of us, humans do not meet up with Giant Squids very often, though there is at least one report from World War Two of survivors of a sunken naval vessel being attacked by a Giant Squid that ate one of the party.

Estimates based on damaged squid carcasses suggest these mighty monsters could reach up to 30 metres across. One story, though, suggests they might get even larger. One night during World War Two, a British Admiralty trawler was lying off the Maldive Islands in the Indian Ocean. One of the crew, A. G. Starkey, was up on deck, alone, fishing, when he saw something in the water.

"As I gazed, fascinated, a circle of green light glowed in my area of illumination. This green unwinking orb I suddenly realized was an eye. The surface of the water undulated with some strange disturbance. Gradually I realized that I was gazing at almost point-blank range at a huge squid." Starkey walked the length the of the ship, finding the tail at one end and the tentacles at the other. The ship was over 50 metres long.

The Colossal Octopus

Known varieties of octopus range in size from a circumference of a few centimetres to as much as seven metres. There is some evidence that, deep in the sea, there lives an unknown species of octopus that can grow to over 30 feet across and weigh ten tonnes.

The octopus is a distant cousin of the squid and both belong to a group of animals called cephalopods. Both are invertebrates, which means they have no backbone, and each has multiple arms, lined with suckers, that allow the creatures to hold fast to prey or other objects. Both are fairly intelligent, with large, dark eyes, and both are carnivorous.

Squid have ten arms, though, while the octopus – as its name suggests – has only eight. Squid are also thought to spend most of their time hovering in the mid-waters while the octopus lives on the ocean floor using its arms to move from rock to rock. Finally, while the squid has a reputation for aggression, the octopus has a more shy and retiring disposition. Only one (dead) Colossal Octopus has ever been found and it was, and still is, surrounded by controversy.

Not that octopi are entirely harmless. When angered, they can be dangerous to both

swimmers and divers. With their strong, long arms they can hold a man underwater until he drowns.

The story starts in November of 1896, when two boys, cycling along the beach in Florida, USA, came across the body of an enormous creature that had been washed up by the tide. Dr DeWitt Webb, a local amateur naturalist and president of the local historical society, took an interest in the remains. After an examination of the mutilated and decaying body, he believed that he'd discovered the carcass of a huge octopus.

The portion of the creature that remained – the body minus the arms – was five and a half metres in length and three metres wide. Parts of tentacles, unattached to the body, stretched as long as eleven metres with a diameter of

25 centimetres. Dr Webb estimated its weight at four or five tons.

Realising this was an important find, Webb wrote to Yale Professor Addison Verrill, a leading expert on cephalopods, about the creature:

"You may be interested to know of the body of an immense Octopus thrown ashore some miles south of this city. Nothing but the stump of the tentacles remains, as it had evidently been dead for some time before being washed ashore."

Based on photographs sent by Webb, Verrill concluded that the creature was indeed a Colossal Octopus that might have had a diameter of 45 metres when living.

Webb finally sent Verrill a sample of the tissue of the creature preserved in formalin.

Verrill was surprised to find it had the appearance of blubber and stated that he now believed the creature was a whale and that the arms were not associated with the body.

The whole matter would have rested like that if it hadn't been for Forrest Wood, the director of Marine Studios in Florida. Wood came across an old news story about the monster and discovered that Webb's sample was still stored at the Smithsonian Institution.

Wood persuaded the Smithsonian to let Dr Joseph Gennaro, of the University of Florida, to take some of the samples for analysis. Gennaro's examination under a microscope showed the tissue was more similar to octopus than whale or squid. Further tests later confirmed this. So it seems that Webb was right and

Verrill changed his mind too quickly. It may take another beached carcass to settle the matter.

A possible Colossal Octopus was recently found off New Zealand's Chatham Islands. The specimen, over four metres in length and weighing 72 kilograms, was picked up in a trawler's net from a depth of 900 metres. The creature has been identified as *Haliphron Atlanticus* – a species of octopus never previously found in the area – by the National Institute of Water and Atmospheric Research.

Because the Colossal Octopus is a bottom dweller, it could be that when the creatures die they stay on the ocean floor and decay, leaving few clues for scientists to find. But as scientists explore the depths of the seas further, we may again come face to face with a Colossal Octopus and look into its huge unblinking eyes.

MONSTOGRAPHY
An A to Z of Mythical Monsters

Aigaumcha

A tiny African monster with eyes on its feet. The Aigaumcha's diet consists of human flesh.

Al

These Armenian monsters have iron teeth, brass claws and eat babies.

Ammut

This is an Egyptian monster with the head of a crocodile, a lion's body and the back end of a hippopotamus. The Egyptians call her the "eater of the dead", because that was her job in the Hall of Double Justice of the god Osiris. The hearts of the dead were weighed against the feather of truth and those that failed to past the test were fed to Ammut.

63

Banshee

The banshee in Irish Gælic is called "bean sidhe". In Scottish, "bean nighe", which means "supernatural woman". She is pictured with a sunken nose, untidy, wild hair and huge, hollow eye sockets. A bean nighe has one prominent tooth, one nostril, long, hanging breasts, and webbed feet. Her eyes are fiery red from continuous weeping. She wears a tattered white sheet and cloak flapping around her, and wails loudly outside the door of someone who is about to die.

Basilisk

A small but deadly reptile, only 15 centimetres long, whose breath is poisonous. In ancient legend was said to possess a glance that would turn any person instantly to stone.

Bobbi-Bobbi

One of the ancestral snakes of the Binbinga people of northern Australia, Bobbi-Bobbi once sent a number of flying foxes (large bats)

for hungry men to eat, but they escaped.
So the snake, watching from his underground
home, threw one of his own ribs up to the
men, who used it as a boomerang to kill the
bats; then they cooked them. Later, however,
they used the boomerang to make a hole in
the sky. This angered the snake, and he
snatched back his rib. Two men who tried
to hang on to it were dragged underground
and eaten alive.

Centaur

The most famous centaurs are those from
Greek mythology. In these myths, the centaurs
are a race of creatures that are half-man and
half-horse. The father of the original centaurs
is the god, Ixion. There are many variations
of the centaur. Some have a human torso
and head on a horse's body. Some are entire
humans with a horse's body and hind legs
stretching back from the waist. Another
variation gives the centaur wings, and
sometimes the centaur's head has horsey ears.

Cerberus

The fearsome three-headed dog of Greek legend who guards the entrance to Hell, Cerberus has a serpent's tail, and is also known as the "Hound of Hades". The mighty Hercules is the only person ever to best him in combat, bringing him back up with him to the world of men for a time, as one of his Twelve Labours.

Cyclops

A man-eating giant who has one eye in the middle of his forehead. In Greek mythology, the Cyclops captured the hero Odysseus, who escaped after he put out the Cyclops' eye.

Dagon

The ancient Philistines, and later the seafaring Phoenicians, considered this half-man half-fish to be their main god. In the Bible it tells that while conquering the Israelites, the Philistines stole the Ark of

the Covenant and placed it before
a statue of Dagon. This shape-shifting
marine god may date back to the ancient
Sumerian god, Oannes, who came from
the ocean to educate mankind.

Damballah
The powerful serpent god of voodoo myth,
he shows himself in the sky above Haiti,
in the Caribbean, appearing with his wife,
Ayida, as a rainbow.

Dragon (Western)
Native Americans believed in snake dragons:
enormous, fire-breathing serpents with scaly
green bodies and huge red wings. Greedy
creatures, they hoard treasure in dens
under the earth. Fierce and hungry,
a dragon is partial to young human flesh.
Dragons live in caves, mountains, or lakes.
They were particularly active in the Middle
Ages in Europe, when brave knights
challenged them in battle.

Dragon (Eastern)

Compared to Western dragons, these beasts are quite small. Their bodies are long, and they have two horns for ears. They have no wings, and their soft breath is said to form clouds. They do not roar; instead they make the sounds of beating gongs and jingling bells. Chinese dragons dine on sparrows. They live wherever there is water. They are kind and wise friends of human beings. At Chinese New Year, dancers don huge dragon costumes and perform special dances in the streets.

Dzoavits

A huge ogre from the myths of the Shoshoneans – a primitive people of Nevada and Utah in the USA. It was conquered by a badger, who lured the mighty giant to a specially prepared hole, threw hot rocks in on him, and then plugged the hole with a boulder, trapping him inside.

Erlking

Erlking is a Germanic goblin who is King of the dwarves. He lures humans, especially children, to the forest and kills them.

Fachen

The Fachen is a monster from Irish legend. He is known to chase and attack travellers, eventually killing them. He is covered with feathers, including a tuft on his head like that of a cockerel. He has one mangled hand that grows from the middle of his chest, and one leg that grows out of his body. He also has one eye set in the middleof his forehead.

Ga-Gorib

In Hottentot myth, this monster would sit on the edge of a great pit and dare passers-by to throw stones at him. The stone always rebounded and killed the thrower, who then fell into the pit to be devoured.

Giant

Albanian giants are as tall as pine trees, with long, black beards. They catch men to eat and women to fan the flies away.

Giants have enormous size and strength packed in a human form. They can roar like thunder, make the earth shake, and snack on grown people. Their characteristics depend on their nationalities. Irish giants are pleasant, English giants are openly evil, and Welsh giants are clever and cunning (for giants). All giants have a keen sense of smell, and use it to sniff out their next victim. Usually their brains are no match for their bodies and they can be outwitted by a smart human. Giants are proof that intelligence is more important than size.

Giantess

Scottish giantesses are known as gruagachs, like their male counterparts. Like most female giants, they are depicted as housewife types who spend their time making bread out of ground-up human bones. Befri, a French giantess, carried off young girls and made them spin thread into cloth. Grendel's mother, in the Norse story of Beowulf, was a mighty ogress who sneaked up on sleeping warriors and ate them 15 at a time.

Goblin

From their birthplace in France, these nasty cousins of gnomes have spread all over Europe. When they entered England in ancient times, the Druids called them Robin Goblins, from which the name "hobgoblin" derives. Goblins have no permanent home, living in old trees and under moss-covered rocks. Playful on occasion, goblins are nonetheless to be avoided. A goblin's smile can curdle blood, and its laugh can turn milk sour. Goblins amuse themselves by hiding things, spilling food, and confusing travellers by changing signposts.

Gorgons

In Greek mythology, the Gorgons were the three daughters of Phorkys and Keto. Their names were Stheino, Euryale and (the most famous) Medusa. They had wings and claws, and snakes instead of hair. Medusa had the power to turn men to stone simply by looking them in the eyes. When she was slain by Perseus, the legendary winged horse Pegasus rose from her fresh blood.

Gnome

The word "gnome" comes from the Greek "gnosis" meaning "knowledge". It was said that they knew where to find precious metals. They are depicted as grotesque dwarves wearing tight-fitting brown clothes and hoods. They live underground and guard the Earth's treasures. Sometimes they are confused with goblins, but gnomes are good-natured, hard-working and reliable, whereas goblins are nasty and spiteful.

Gremlin

Gremlins were born in the United States. Highly mechanical, they have been responsible for much technological progress. They live around tools and inside machines and appliances. During World War Two, however, gremlins turned against mankind, after human mechanics and scientists began to take credit for gremlin work. They started to cause mechanical failures in aircrafts, motor vehicles and other mechanical devices, and gremlins are blamed for technical glitches of all kinds to this day.

Harpies

The Harpies were loathsome monsters employed by the gods to punish crime on Earth. They were three sisters with the bodies of birds and the heads of women, with trunks like elephants. Always ravenous, they would punish wrongdoers by stealing their food and leaving them to starve.

Hippogryph

The hippogryph is a cross between a male gryphon and a filly. It has the head, wings and front legs of a gryphon, and the body and hind legs of a horse. It is a powerful creature that can move through the air with astonishing speed. It figured in several of the legends of Charlemagne as a mount for some of his knights.

Ichthyocentaur

The Ichthyocentaur is a variation of the centaur. Living in the sea, it has the upper half of a man, the tail of a dolphin and the forelegs of a horse or lion.

Jinshin-uwo

The source of all Japanese earthquakes, this thousand-metre-long eel carries Japan on its back. By lashing its large tail, the Jinshin-uwo, or "earthquake fish", causes the ground above to rumble and shake.

Kappa

An ugly green monster from Japan with a monkey's head and a turtle's shell, it drags people into its watery home to eat them.

Leprechaun

Leprechauns are small fairies from Irish folklore. Grotesque in appearance, dressed in green with leather aprons, silver-buckled shoes, red caps, and spectacles on the end of their noses, leprechauns are famous for being shoemakers. But a leprechaun will never make a pair of shoes: he will make just one shoe at a time. They like to play tricks on humans but if a leprechaun is caught by a human (which is very difficult to accomplish), he is forced to reveal the location of his hidden treasure, usually gold. While he is guiding you to his treasure, you must watch him very closely – if you take your eyes off him for a single second, he will vanish into thin air.

Lernaean Hydra

A fearsome beast from Greek mythology with nine heads, whose very breath and smell is deadly poison to mortal men. Eight of the Hydra's heads are mortal; the ninth is impossible to kill.

Kraken

The Kraken, which is found in Scandinavian myth, is a huge sea creature. It is said to lie at the bottom of the sea for long periods of time and then surface, when sailors mistake the creature's many humps for a chain of small islands, sometimes even landing on one and building a camp, only to be drowned when the creature submerges once more. The Kraken is supposed to have enormous tentacles, which can seize even the largest ships and drag them, and all on board, to a watery grave.

Logaroo

Like vultures by day, these mythical Caribbean creatures shed their skin at night, hide in fog, and suck blood from the lost victims they catch.

Lung

The rainbringing dragons of Chinese folklore. The Lung were called upon in ancient times to refresh the Earth with their waters. The Lung can make themselves as small as silkworms, or become so large that they can overshadow the entire world. They are composed of many parts of different animals. The horns of a stag sit on the head of a camel, with the eyes of a demon and the neck of a snake. They are covered in the scales of a fish, and have the claws of an eagle, the pads of a tiger, the ears of a bull and the whiskers of a cat.

Manticora

From the West Indies, the Manticora is a lion with human features and eyes that burn blue fire; it can shoot deadly quills from its tail.

Minotaur

A half-man half-bull monster from the island of Crete, the Minotaur is the son of the Queen, Pasiphae, and a bull sent to her by the sea god, Poseidon. Her husband, Minos, built a labyrinth (maze) on the island to contain his monstrous stepson. The Minotaur, usually pictured as having a human body and a bull's head, ate human flesh. It was sent seven boys and seven girls every year as a sacrifice, to stop it from leaving Crete to terrorise the world at large.

New Jersey Devil

An American monster that is part ram, part kangaroo with bat wings, a horse's feet, and a pointed tail. It feeds on barnyard animals.

Nixie

Nixies are Germanic sprites who live in water. Although the male doesn't often show himself to humans, the female is often seen sitting in the sun on the banks of rivers and lakes. Nixie maidens are beautiful with long hair and blue eyes. If a man tries to spy on their beauty, their song can cause him to go mad.

O Goncho

A dragon from Japan. Every 50 years this white beast turns into a golden bird. Its cry signifies the coming of famine.

Oni

The Oni are Japanese demons. In Shinto legend, they are associated with disease, calamity and misfortune. These interfering spirits are basically human in shape, but possess three eyes, a wide mouth, horns, and three sharp talons on both hands and feet. Oni can fly, often swooping down to seize the soul of a wicked man who is about to die.

Ovda

An unfriendly forest spirit, Ovda wanders in the woods of Finland as a naked human being with its feet turned backwards. Sometimes it appears as a man, sometimes a woman. Ovda entices its victims by challenging them to dance; then it tickles them to death.

Ping Feng

A huge, pig-like beast from China, Ping Feng has a head at each end, and attacks people and large animals.

Pixie

No larger than a human hand, a pixie is human-like with red hair and green eyes. They have upturned noses and mischievous smiles. They wear tight-fitting green clothes. Pixies can change their size at will. They are tricksters who like to lead humans astray, and are usually found in the English counties of Somerset, Devon, and Cornwall.

Some farmers embrace the presence of pixies and do certain things to keep them on the farm, leaving a bucket of water out so mother pixies can wash their babies, and milk for them to drink. They will also sweep the hearth so that the pixies have a clean place to dance.

Questing Beast

The Questing Beast has a snake's head, a leopard's body and a lion's back end with the paws of a hare, or a deer's hooves. It is continually seeking water to slake its unquenchable thirst. As it runs, its belly makes the sound of a pack of hounds. It appears several times in the legends of King Arthur.

Rakshasa

An ogre who lives in a palace in India. His gold and jewels make him rich, but he is filthy and quite stupid. Like all ogres, he enjoys eating people. He can appear in many ugly shapes, coming from nowhere to kill his victims with a single scratch from his poisonous tail.

Redcap

Redcaps are malevolent goblins, easily distinguishable by their red hats and fiery red eyes. Their caps are red because they dip them in the blood of their human victims. Redcaps wear iron boots, but are quick on their feet. They live in castles along the English-Scottish border. They have sharp eagle's talons with which they kill their victims. Short and stocky, redcaps have long white beards and look like old men. Just as with goblins, all that is needed to keep them at bay is the use of certain well-chosen holy words.

Sasabonsam

A monster from Ashanti myth, the Sasabonsam is a hairy beast with large, bloodshot eyes, long legs and feet pointing both ways. Its favourite trick is to sit in the high branches of a tree and dangle its long legs, so as to entrap unwary hunters.

Scorpion Men

From ancient Sumerian legend, Scorpion Men are born of the god Tiamat along with the viper, dragon, sphinx, great lion and mad dog. They are human from the waist up and scorpion from the waist down. The astrological constellation, Scorpio, comes from this creature. It was often depicted as a guard in the city of Babylon.

Tiamat

The dreaded dragon of Babylonian legend, Tiamat was said to be revolting in appearance, being a cross between a bird, a serpent and an animal, and she was seen as utterly evil. Tiamat was eventually defeated by the god, Marduk, who shot a raging wind into her mouth, so that she could not close it and swallow him, then shot an arrow into her belly, slaying her. Marduk then created the heavens and Earth out of her dead body.

Troll

In Norse mythology, trolls are known as dim-witted gigantic man-eating creatures who live in caves in the mountains. They are ugly and quite evil. Trolls would be turned to stone if they were hit by the sun's rays. They guard treasure and are good at metal-working. In later legends, trolls are smaller, dwarf-like beings who still live in caves but are not as strong or bloodthirsty as their predecessors. They still like to steal women and children, though, and are cleverer than their forefathers.

Sleipnir

In Viking mythology, this horse was the steed of the god Odin (from whom we get the word Wednesday). This grey horse had eight legs and could run faster than the wind. It could fly in the air, run on the earth and dive down into the regions of hell.

89

Unicorn

The first mention of the unicorn came from the Roman Ctesias in 389 BC: he said that it was a wild beast similar to a horse. Pure in spirit, with white bodies, red heads and blue eyes, unicorns have a single ivory horn on their heads.

Wishpoosh

According to the Nez Perce Indians of Washington, the beaver monster Wishpoosh refused to allow anyone to fish. Whenever a person came to the lake where he lived, he would seize them with his huge claws and drag them underwater.

Wyvern

Appearing quite often in heraldry, the Wyvern is a snake-like dragon with wings. It has two legs with talons like an eagle and a tail that ends in a point like an arrowhead. The Wyvern symbolises war, pestilence, envy and viciousness.

Yuki Onna

The Yuki Onna, or Snow Woman, is a Japanese female demon that inhabits snowstorms and causes travellers to become lost. Eventually the weary trekkers become exhausted and freeze to death.

Ziz

A bird mentioned in the book of Psalms in the Bible, the Ziz is a bird of enormous size. It can block out the sun with its wings and has incredible strength. It is said that it was created to protect all small birds, and without its protection, these birds would have died a long time ago. When roasted, it is also said to be a delicacy for gigantic banquets.

Zombie

Followers of some branches of Haitian and West African voodoo believe a spirit or spell can bring a corpse back to life to perform evil deeds for its master. These are zombies: they walk like robots and can be made to do anything for their masters, from manual labour to murder.

FANGS FOR THE MEMORY

A Brief History of Vampires

In 1047, the first appearance of the word "upir" (an early form of the word which later became "vampire") was in a document referring to a Russian prince as "upir lichy", or "wicked vampire".

In around 1250, **several suspected cases of vampirism were reported in the East European country of Moravia, now part of the Czech Republic. Reports circulated that a vampire was leaving its tomb in the local cemetery and attacking sleeping women and children. Those who had seen the vampire said it was a leading citizen of the community who had recently died. A "vampire hunter" was summoned from neighbouring Hungary.**

The story goes that the vampire hunter climbed up the church tower overlooking the cemetery and kept watch. When the man saw the vampire emerge from his tomb and disappear into the town, he hurried down and stole a shroud from the open coffin. When the vampire returned and found its shroud missing, it looked up at the tower which the hunter had reclimbed and began to howl with an unearthly voice. The man challenged the creature to come up the tower and retrieve its shroud. The vampire hunter kept his nerve until the creature had almost reached him, then knocked it off the building with a shovel. Before the vampire could recover from the fall, the man descended and cut off its head with the shovel.

In 1310, King Philip of France ordered that the corpse of a certain Jehan de Turo be dug up and destroyed by fire "on suspicion that he was a vampire".

In 1451, **at Gratz in the mountainous regions of upper Styria, now a province of Austria, lived Barbara de Cilly, a beautiful woman much loved by one Sigismund of Hungary. When close to death, her life was apparently saved by a secret ritual devised by Abramerlin the Mage, but as a result was condemned forever after to be a vampire. She became the inspiration for *Camilla*, a vampire novel by the Irish writer, Joseph Sheridan Le Fanu.**

In 1560, Elizabeth Bathory, later known as the "Blood Countess", was born. She was arrested in 1610 for killing several hundred people and bathing in their blood. Tried and convicted, she was sentenced to life imprisonment. She was bricked into a room in her castle, where she died in 1614.

In 1734, **the word "vampyre" entered the English language after German accounts of waves of vampire hysteria. In 1798, Samuel Taylor Coleridge wrote** Christabel, **now believed to be the first vampire poem in English.**

In 1810, reports circulated through northern England of sheep being killed by having their jugular veins cut and their blood drained.

In 1819, **Dr John Polidori's** The Vampyre, **the first vampire story in English, was published in** New Monthly Magazine. **It was entered for the same writing competition for which Mary Shelley wrote** Frankenstein, **and its central character, Lord Ruthven, was modelled after the famous poet Lord Byron. Many were convinced Byron had penned the tale himself, based on his own vampiric experiences.**

In 1845, after the death of Horace Ray in Jewett City, Connecticut, USA, the members of his family all fell ill with a wasting disease. When just one sickly son remained alive, the father's body was dug up from its grave and found to be as fresh as the day it had been laid to rest. After the corpse was burned, the health of the surviving son improved and he lived to a ripe old age, convinced that his dad had indeed been a vampire.

In 1872, **in Italy, Vincenzo Verzeni was convicted of murdering two people and drinking their blood.**

In 1897, Bram Stoker's novel, *Dracula*, revived the story of Vlad the Impaler for the modern world. Considered by many scholars to be the most bloodthirsty full-length book in English literature, it has never gone out of print and remains a bestseller. Sadly, Stoker never lived to see *Dracula's* phenomenal success. He died in 1912, a poor and unrecognised man.

Also in 1897, **another novel, entitled** *The Vampire,* **created in detail the vampire character we recognise on stage and in hundreds of movies ever since. It was written by Rudyard Kipling, who also wrote the book on which the Disney movie** *The Jungle Book* **was based.**

In 1921, the remains of a suspected vampire were found in Essex, England. A skeleton believed to be that of a woman, which was found in St Osyth, is thought to have been buried as a vampire. As custom decreed, the remains had been bound with rope, and nails had been driven through the thigh bones to prevent it from rising from the grave after death.

In 1958, **Hammer Films in Great Britain started a new wave of interest in vampires with the first of its** *Dracula* **films.**

In 1964, *The Munsters* and *The Addams Family* – two horror comedies with vampire characters – were first shown on American TV.

In 1992, **Andrei Chikatilo of Rostov, Russia, was sentenced to death after killing and "vampirizing" 55 people.**

In 1996, members of a vampire cult led by Rod Ferrell were arrested for the murder of two people in Florida, USA. They were subsequently tried and convicted of the murders.

In 1997, **celebrations marked a hundred years since the publication of Bram Stoker's novel** *Dracula*. **These led to Dracula-related books, TV shows and the release of commemorative postage stamps in Canada, Ireland, England and the United States.**

UNLUCKY DIP

Miscellaneous Monstrosities

After Nelson's death at the Battle of Trafalgar in 1805, his body is thought to have been preserved in a barrel of rum or brandy for the trip home

The ghost of a famous Japanese samurai warrior named Masakado Taira has his own bank account worth more than £120,000. Although Taira died 1,000 years ago, Tokyo residents still leave food, gifts and money at his stone monument located in the heart of the city's financial district. Managing Taira's funds, and everything else related to the spirit, is a man called Tatsuzo Endo, chairman of the Masakado Preservation Society, who admits, "I'm not really sure ghosts need money."

The word "Pokemon" is an abbreviation of "pocket monster". In Japan the word "poke" is used to mean something small. The video game was launched in 1996 in Japan by Satoshi Tajira, and the craze spread to trading cards, comic books, a television series, films and toys, with sales running into billions of dollars. Officially there were only 150 species of Pokemon, but unknown to the manufacturers, Nintendo, Tajira hid a 151st in the software, the rare and powerful Mew.

Frankenstein's castle actually exists. It is located in Darmstadt in Germany. But the mad scientist who lived there and performed the experiments wasn't a Dr Frankenstein, but one Konrad Johann Dippel. He occupied the castle in the 17th century, using corpses from the local cemetery to experiment on. When the townspeople started to suspect him

of stealing corpses, he stopped using them and started trying the experiments on himself. He later died after drinking one of his own potions.

The Tibetans used to have a novel way of keeping their lamas, or spiritual leaders, with them after death. First, the body of the departed was packed with lacquer-saturated padding. Then it was wrapped in lacquered silk and placed in a seated position in a hot room filled with salt. After several days of drying, it was cooled down, then covered all over with gold leaf and placed on a throne with the other gilded lamas.

The Ancient Incas of Peru preserved dead bodies with a combination of aromatic oils and slow drying.

Alexander the Great's body was preserved in honey.

When St John of the Cross died in 1591, he was buried in a vault beneath the floor of a church in Ubeda, Spain. When the tomb was opened nine months later, his body was said to be fresh and intact; and when a finger was removed to use as a holy relic, it bled like that of a living person. The body was exhumed again in 1859, and again said to be in perfect condition, 250 years after his death.

In Haiti, the poison found in the glands of puffer fish is used in a powder for making "zombies". It brings on a state of paralysis so complete that although the person is alive, they seem dead, even to a doctor. The puffer fish is also eaten in Japan as a very expensive delicacy, carved by chefs specially trained to ensure no poison is left on the diner's plate. Mistakes do occur however, and people still die every year from eating this dangerous treat.

"Teratophobia" is the fear of monsters.

A person born on Halloween is reputedly able to see and talk to spirits.

Vampire bats don't suck blood. They make a small incision in an animal's skin and lap up the oozing blood with their tongues.

In East Africa, soccer teams hire witch doctors to ensure their success. Known as "jujumen", these soothsaying specialists use a variety of magical rituals to create successful outcomes for their teams. In fact, witchcraft is considered part of the team's mental preparation for a game; just knowing that a jujuman is using divine powers helps team members relax. Typical witchcraft prescriptions include avoiding women first thing in the morning and leaving soccer balls on a grave during the night before a big game.

If you fancy following in the footsteps of the ancient Egyptians and becoming a mummy after your own death, you can. Summum, a religious group in Salt Lake City, Utah, USA, will do the mummification for $63,000. The modern technique involves being soaked for six months in a secret formula of preservation fluid, dozens of coats of polyurethane rubber, and layers of fibreglass bandages. Your mummified body is then sealed into a bronze case with resin, pharoah-style.

In 1982, *Empire* magazine published a letter written by a woman from Colorado, USA. She claimed that in 1935, when she was a young child, she saw five baby dinosaurs. A few months after she saw them a farmer shot one. The woman saw the body, and said it was "about seven feet tall, was grey, had a head like a snake, short front legs with claws that resembled chicken feet, large stout back legs, and a long tail."

Before becoming the most famous Frankenstein's Monster on our movie screens, actor Boris Karloff was an estate agent.

Traditionally, individuals with a natural squint, as well as dwarfs and hunchbacks, are considered to have the evil-eye: able to cause harm to victims just with a look. Curiously, in Mediterranean lands, blue-eyed folks are more likely to be accused of possessing an evil stare, while in northern Europe, dark-eyed people are more suspect.

The infamous Black Death in Europe was due in part to the fact that people believed cat owners to be witches. All the cats were rounded up, caged and burned, leaving the rats (with their disease-causing parasites) to run free and multiply. Those secretly harbouring cats were among the ones who survived.

In the Trang area of Thailand, locals believe that evil spirits are causing a stream of fatal car accidents. The troubled stretch of road is known as the "100 corpses crossroads" and has created commotion and concern all the way to the highest levels of government. One Thai politician has asked for local monks to conduct a religious ceremony to help improve safety. Spirits of the dead victims are also being asked to help guard the area.

Some people believe that objects that have been in contact with each other have a psychic link, and that their personal possessions will forever be psychically joined with them. That's why a witch is extra-anxious when a personal belonging goes missing: she's fearful that the item that once touched her body could be used in a nasty spell against her.

According to ancient tradition, to protect your home from evil spirits on Halloween, you must walk around your house three times backwards and anti-clockwise before sunset.

Beneath the streets of Paris lie catacombs of bones. Six million people are buried there, their bones arranged as walls. Skulls are arranged as crosses, and form entire archways. Trips through the mass graves have been on offer to brave tourists.

In Thailand, the bodies of monks are preserved in the belief that the purity of their souls in life has assured that their earthly remains are pure. These monks are on public display and are objects of worship. No special techniques are said to be used to preserve the bodies, yet they decay very slowly even in an atmosphere of smog, humidity, and heat. They still have teeth, hair, and skin, decades after their deaths.

If you enjoyed this book, you can find more amazing facts in the following books:

Title	ISBN
1000 of the World's Most Astonishing Facts	0603560679
The World's Most Amazing Animal Facts for Kids	0603560601
The World's Most Amazing Battle Facts for Kids	0603560989
The World's Most Amazing Crime Facts for Kids	0603560970
The World's Most Amazing Inventions Facts for Kids	0603560997
The World's Most Amazing Planet Earth Facts for Kids	0603560628
The World's Most Amazing Science Facts for Kids	060356061X

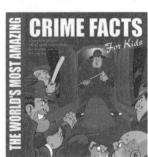